"I know I have to start over,
but why now?"

Instant Tears for Lovers

Sandy Kelley

Illustrated by Claudia Ricketts

Celestial Arts
Millbrae, Ca 94030

First Printing, April 1974
Library of Congress Card No.: 73-86639
ISBN 0-912310-51-0 Paper Edition
Made in the United States of America

I.

Alone

I am going to catch
a ride on the wind
and blow into your dreams,
warm and naked,
ready for your touch . . .

Will you let me stay,
at least for the night?

Listen to the wind
Blowing in the window
And singing in the curtains.
It has killed the
Glow from the candle
You gave me
That smells like pine.

Wind always reminds
Me of your love,
Entering the room,
Rearranging everything
In its path;
And then, leaving,
Selfishly, just
When I begin to
Enjoy its
Gentle breeze.

Perhaps I
Will close
The window.

DON'T GO

If you're going to leave me
   leave me now
while I can still remember
the feel of your hands
on my breast.

Leave me something to
   remember you by —
if only the memory of
your smile when you were
satisfied with our
lovemaking.

If you must go,
   go now
while the yellow roses
are still in bloom.
Roses are so much a
part of our love.
Each night I spent with you
will be a Yellow Rose Night
in my memory.

If you must leave me,
   leave me now —
before my dreams give
way to reality,
before my tears betray
my broken heart.

        Please, don't leave me,
          not now.

I know I have to start over
        but why now?

Why can't I just stay in bed
        and pretend
        today
        is still
        yesterday
                until tomorrow?

Perhaps tomorrow you will return
        and
starting over will be unnecessary

        for awhile.

Anything can happen
in dreams.

Anything can happen
in love.

Yet, you must
wake up
from both

alone.

The parks are
full of people
seeking escape
        from other people.

THE WIND

The wind has a way
of calling me to follow—
   blowing in my window, whispering
   my name, softly, so that only
   I can hear . . .
   Promising me adventure, found
   only in freedom, if I will
   but follow the wind.
And yet,
   I stay beneath the safety
   of my own roof—
   afraid to trade the reality
   of knowing for the
   fantasy of dreams,
     afraid to follow the
     wind in search of freedom.
I am content
to pull the covers
over my head and
play dead
   while the wind races
   forward, seeking
   a new life,
     without me . . .

Avoid using
the word
. . .love
for one
short day

and discover
how long
one night
can seem . . .

II.

Both of Us

Silently, I spend the night alone,
except for thoughts of yesterday
when you were near—
                    I miss you.

Softly, I remember the smell
of your body after our
afternoon of love making—
a fragrance that drives me
wild, even tonight—
                    I miss you.

Sadly, I seek refuge from
thoughts in the dark,
praying for a loss of memory
to replace my love for you—
                    I miss you.

A touch can mean
so many things:

Come
be my love,
share the new day
with me
as the sun comes
up over tomorrow.

A touch can be
an invitation
to happiness.

Touch me with
your smile.

What do you know about me?
I mean really know about me?

Do you know the color yellow
really turns me on?
And I always wear black
to a wedding?

Do you know my favorite foods
are dill pickles and crackers?
And I hate Broccoli
if its chopped up?

Do you know I am
afraid at night?
Of myself more
than the boogeyman?

Do you know I hate
birthdays?
And love to play
monopoly in bed?

What do you know about me?
I mean really know about me?

It's after you make love to me
I am sure of our love—
Lying beside you in the dark,
feeling my body throb with
the aftermath of our love,
I have a chance to examine
with reason, all the emotions
you proclaimed in the
heat of our passion—

        Only then do I realize the
        height of our ecstasy,
        or the depth behind our
        need to unite in unity.

You hold me in your arms and
stroke my matted hair
with the assurance
found only in satisfaction.
I glow from an inner-
beauty inspired from
being just right for another.
Total relaxation controls
our bodies with happiness.

        This is the time I await.
        Our need becomes want—
        Our lust becomes love.
        Mentally we truly become one,
        pledging our love for eternity.
        And we unite without reservations.

I never meant for it to
happen this way,
        but it did . . .
Now, I need you:
        to want me
        to love me
        to hold me.
It's not an easy
confession for me to make,
        needing someone else,
                but I do . . .
Before you, I shared my
life only with the cat:
        we understood each other
        we asked nothing of each other
        we gave only at will.
Independence was
a private word
belonging only to me
before you came
upon the scene:
        now you exist
        now you rate
        now you are
                the answer to my
                every question
        the clock to
        time my day
                the companion I
                seek for night
        the reason for
        living my life
                the dream I never
                meant to come true,
        but you did—
or, am I
still dreaming?

HEAVEN

talk to me
share my warmth
drift inside of me
touch my smile
   and float
   silently
   above the clouds
   gliding
   peacefully
together . . .

if you look closely,
you can see my flaws—

     I
     am
     created
     of
     imperfections

     which
     makes
     me
     a
     perfect
     woman . . .

I know I'm
different
from other
people—

that's what
I like
most about
myself.

There is no winning
without losing—

So, the most I can
gain in loving you
is the giving
of myself,

And yet, I love you
without reservations.
I give you me
in exchange for us.

I didn't mean to love you
but my need was great
and there you were . . .
                    waiting
                    looking,
with needs of your own
                    to be fulfilled.
I only meant to care about you
as I would any man searching.
My only desire was to see you smile,
    blue eyes were not meant for tears . . .

I didn't mean to love you
but you were there
and so was I . . .
                    waiting
                    looking
for someone to love . . .

BE SURE

Before you tell me
of your love,
be sure.

> My
> sanity
> depends
> on
> your
> sincerity.

I identify love
with a non-returnable bottle,

once you have used the contents
it's only good for polluting
the environment.

I can use an empty bottle
for a flower vase—

I have no use
for an empty heart.

FACTS OF LIFE

You will be remembered
as a fact of my life,
like my height
       or weight
              or the color
              of my eyes.

Your loving me
was a fact
nicer to remember
than even the Christmas
Santa brought my first bike.

Your leaving
was also
a fact,

       followed by the
       fact you would
       never return—

Still, you were
a part of my life . . .

              even a fact
              can't last
                     forever.

This morning
    you were only
    the dream of
        yesterday.

This afternoon,
    you have become
    the memory of
        tomorrow.

From my window, I watch a young
couple working in their yard.
She, with her belly swelled with
the evidence of procreation.
Him, smiling at the afternoon sun
as though he were a youth again,
in spite of the added responsibility
associated with fatherhood.
They play like children, laughing
and loving the warm sunshine,
ignoring the wind blowing under
her short maternity top, showing
off the pregnancy with pride.

As I watch, I remember . . .
yesterday, you, and yes, even us.
What happened to our sunshine days?
         I am still fertile with
         love, despite my age—
         Look into my eyes, for
         they reveal the evidence
         of your manhood . . .
                  My spring is over,
                  even summer has
                  passed for me—
                  but a fall garden
                  still flourishes
                  with attention.

you undress me
with your eyes,
    leaving me hungry
    for your touch . . .

YOU'VE HAD IT!

Well, you've really done it now!
    Teaching me to
    enjoy the warm
    sweet smell of
    another body
    next to my own
    was bad enough—
But you had to go even farther.
    Now look what
    you've gone and done!
    I'm in love with you.
    Okay, laugh. I would
    have laughed too,
    a few weeks ago.
    but not now!
    My love is true
    enough today
    to be a fact—
You've really done it now,

    Lover . . .

DEE

Running away from love
is not as simple
as you might think.

You think you can
just forget him,
but yesterdays
return when today's
sun gives way
to the night—

Escape is not
so easy
in the dark . . .

You trip over
too many
obstacles
called memories.

Because the night
produced a violent
thunderstorm,
the morning gave
birth to a
rainbow—

forgive me . . .

PLEASE

Believe me.
Always
        Believe me.
Even though you
don't always
understand the
why of my how,
believe in my
effort to
please you.

Believe that
I care.
        Believe me.
No matter how
well I imitate
an island,
my need for
you is very real.
Take pride in
your importance
in my life.

Believe that
I love you.
        Believe me.
If the time
ever dawns that
you distrust all
else about me,
believe in
my love—

        That's all I
        really believe
        about my self—
                just you . . .

you clutter
my mind with
thoughts
of love . . .

Sometimes at night
when I am sure no
one is watching me,
. . . I cry.
  Does that surprise you?
      or disappoint you?

ME

Today, I brought you a
      six pack of Coors
      and a woman to love,
              me—

See, it's not just your
      mind that interests
             me.

Today
reminds me of another day
when you took me to the park—
   We spent the day
   swinging in the wind
   and laughing at the sun.

Today
is that kind of day—
   warm, with a springtime sun
   yet, kissed with a gentle
                  breeze . . .

The only thing missing is
                you—
   Winter must have
   scared you away . . .

"US"

Come on, walk me to the car
        past the group of
        young males standing
        in the parking lot,
I want to show you off—
        Let them see the
        real reason behind
        this wiggle in my
        butt, besides
        I don't feel like
        phony smiles today—
        not after "us" . . .

OUR WORLD

We met in the park
because we had no
other place to go—
Besides, it seemed
the obvious place
for two people in
love to spend a
sunny, spring day.
You took my hand
in yours and raced
me across the gentle
grass to the waiting
wonder of the swings.

Laughter was the only
audible sound as
we zoomed upward
to the clouds.
We played as we
loved, together—
sharing the day
with memories of
our childhood,
giving our love
freely to fill the
void left from
growing up—
capturing the
happiness of
both generations,

our own world.

How
beautiful
am
I
when
your
hands
decorate
my
face.

I
prove
my
love
for
you
with
each
new
day
by
beginning
again.

your smell remains
with me long after
you are gone—
    the perfume of
    your body mingled
    with my own
    stays with me
    for hours
filling my head
with thoughts
of togetherness
    but a warm bath
    laced with
    bubbles of
    lavender
    and the smell
    of you is
    forgotten
if only memories
could be washed
away as easily
and replaced with
the fragrance
of spring flowers . . .

Loving
you
means
spending
Saturday
night
alone . . .

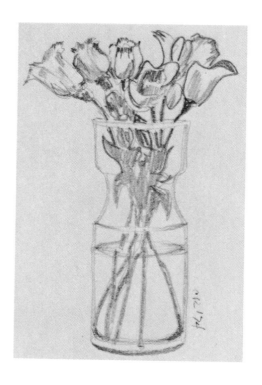

I can no more explain
the why of loving you
than I can explain the
need for stars on a moonlight
                    night . . .

I love you because
you open the gate and
let me in when I have
no place to go.

I love you because
you do not lie to
me about the picture
beside your bed.

I love you because
you let me talk about
me when you need
to hear about you.

I love you because
you make me laugh just
when I'm sure there's
nothing to laugh about.

I love you because
you remind me to
eat even though
I'm not hungry—

I love you because
you eat with me
even though you
are not hungry.

I love you because
you continue to
put us before
you put yourself.

I love you because
you ask no sensible
explanation as to why
                I love you . . .

I am
                looking
                searching
                waiting
        for someone special
        to come along
who is
                looking
                searching
                waiting
        for someone special
        to come along . . .

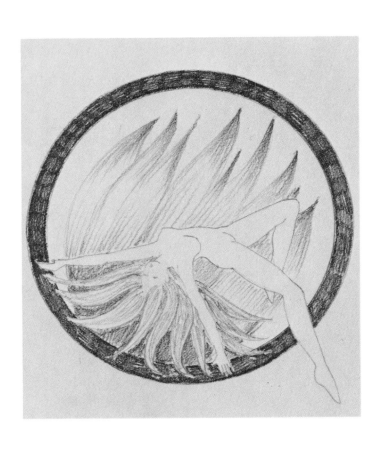

you don't
have to die
and go to Hell
to discover fire—

try love . . .

THE END

this poem is not
going to be
about you—

this poem is not
going to be
about love—

this poem is
going to be
different—

this poem is not
going to be . . .

CELESTIAL ARTS BOOK LIST

LOVE IS AN ATTITUDE. The world-famous book of poetry and photographs by Walter Rinder. 128 pages, clothbound. $6.95; paperbound, $3.95.

THIS TIME CALLED LIFE. Poetry and photography by Walter Rinder. 160 pages, clothbound, $6.95; paperbound, $3.95.

SPECTRUM OF LOVE. Walter Rinder's remarkable love poem with magnificently enhancing drawings by David Mitchell. 64 pages, clothbound, $5.95; paperbound, $2.95

FOLLOW YOUR HEART. A new and powerful companion to the fabulously successful Spectrum of Love with illustrations by Richard Davis. 64 pages, clothbound, $5.95. paperbound, $2.95.

THE HUMANNESS OF YOU. Walt Rinder philosophy and art rendered in his own words and photographs. 64 pages, paperbound, $2.95.

GROWING TOGETHER. George and Donni Betts' poetry with photographs by Robert Scales. 128 pages, paperbound, $3.95.

VISIONS OF YOU. Poems by George Betts, with photographs by Robert Scales. 128 pages, paperbound, $3.95.

MY GIFT TO YOU. New poems by George Betts, with photographs by Robert Scales. 128 pages, paperbound, $3.95.

YOU & I. Leonard Nimoy, the distinguished actor, blends his poetry and photography into a beautiful love story. 96 pages, clothbound, $5.95; paperbound, $2.95.

SPEAK THEN OF LOVE. Deep and sensitive poems from Andrew Oerke with beautifully illustrated drawings from ancient Asian texts. 80 pages, paperbound, $3.95.

WILD BIRDS AND OTHERS. Poetry rich in imagry and depth of compassion from Wendy Long. Beautiful photographs by Ron Sugiyama. 80 pages, paperbound, $2.95

WHERE DO YOU GO FROM HERE? Poignant, funny, always moving, one-liners in a circus of photographs by Robert Weston. 64 pages, paperbound, $2.95.

I AM. Concepts of awareness in poetic form by Michael Grinder. Illustrated in color by Chantal. 64 pages, paperbound, $2.95.

SONG TO THEE, DIVINE ANDROGYNE (Seven Steps to Heaven). A Psalm of Praise for the new age integrating modern psychology with ancient religion by Rowena Pattee. 128 pages, paperbound, $3.95.

GAMES STUDENTS PLAY (And what to do about them.) A study of Transactional Analysis in Schools, by Kenneth Ernst. 128 pages, clothbound, $6.95; paperbound, $3.95.

A GUIDE FOR SINGLE PARENTS (Transactional Analysis for People in Crisis.) T.A. for single parents by Kathern Hallett. 128 pages, clothbound, $6.95; paperbound, $3.95.

THE PASSIONATE MIND (A Manual for Living Creatively with One's Self.) Guidance and understanding from Joel Kramer. 128 pages, paperbound, $3.95.

DREAMS: Messages From My Self. A sensitive effort aimed at helping individuals appreciate and interpret their own dreams by Ruth Kramer. 80 pages, paperbound, $2.95.

THE SENSIBLE BOOK (A Celebration of Your Five Senses.) Barbara Polland awakens the understanding of their senses for children. 64 pages, paperbound, $3.95.

THE LIBERATED MOTHER GOOSE. A bold stroke in behalf of the re-education of children and their parents from Tamar Hoffs. 128 pages, paperbound, $3.95.

THE SPORTS TIME MACHINE. Newslike text and pictures of the great moments in the history of sports by Dave Brase and Tim Simons. 96 pages, paperbound, $2.95.